CLAYTON

D0820675

Pebble®

Exotic Cats

WITHDRAWN

by **Connie Colwell Miller**

Consulting Editor: Gail Saunders-Smith, PhD

Consultant: Jennifer Zablotny, DVM
Member, American Veterinary Medical Association

CONTRA COSTA COUNTY LIBRARY

3 1901 03715 1760

Capstone
press®
Mankato, Minnesota

Pebble Books are published by Capstone Press,
151 Good Counsel Drive, P.O. Box 669, Mankato, Minnesota 56002.
www.capstonepress.com

Copyright © 2009 by Capstone Press, a Capstone Publishers company.
All rights reserved.
No part of this publication may be reproduced in whole or in part,
or stored in a retrieval system, or transmitted in any form or by any means,
electronic, mechanical, photocopying, recording, or otherwise,
without written permission of the publisher.
For information regarding permission, write to Capstone Press,
151 Good Counsel Drive, P.O. Box 669, Dept. R, Mankato, Minnesota 56002.
Printed in the United States of America

1 2 3 4 5 6 13 12 11 10 09 08

Library of Congress Cataloging-in-Publication Data
Miller, Connie Colwell, 1976–
    Exotic cats / by Connie Colwell Miller.
    p. cm. — (Pebble Books. Cats)
    Includes bibliographical references and index.
    Summary: "Simple text and photographs present an introduction to the
Exotic breed, its growth from kitten to adult, and pet care information" — Provided
by publisher.
    ISBN-13: 978-1-4296-1714-7 (hardcover)
    ISBN-10: 1-4296-1714-4 (hardcover)
    1. Exotic shorthair cat — Juvenile literature. I. Title.
SF449.E93M55 2009
636.8 — dc22   2007051272

Note to Parents and Teachers

The Cats set supports national science standards related to life
science. This book describes and illustrates Exotic cats. The images
support early readers in understanding the text. The repetition of
words and phrases helps early readers learn new words. This book
also introduces early readers to subject-specific vocabulary words,
which are defined in the Glossary section. Early readers may need
assistance to read some words and to use the Table of Contents,
Glossary, Read More, Internet Sites, and Index sections of the book.

Table of Contents

Gentle Cats

Exotic cats are
gentle and quiet.

Exotics have
round heads
and small, flat noses.

Exotics' short coats
are thick and soft.
They feel like
cuddly teddy bears.

From Kitten to Adult

All Exotics are born
with short fur.
Exotic kittens sometimes
grow long coats.

Exotic kittens are
born with blue eyes.
Their big round eyes
turn copper-brown
as they grow.

Exotics are fully grown
at 2 years old.
They can weigh up to
15 pounds (7 kilograms).

Caring for Exotics

Exotics need
food and water
every day.

Exotics may have
runny eyes.
Owners need to clean
around Exotics' eyes gently.

Exotics enjoy being
with their owners.
These cats
make great pets.

Glossary

coat — an animal's hair or fur

copper — a reddish brown color

gentle — kind and calm

owner — a person who has something; pets need owners who care for them.

Read More

Barnes, Julia. *Pet Cats*. Pet Pals. Milwaukee: Gareth Stevens, 2007.

Shores, Erika L. *Caring for Your Cat*. Positively Pets. Mankato, Minn.: Capstone Press, 2007.

Internet Sites

FactHound offers a safe, fun way to find Internet sites related to this book. All of the sites on FactHound have been researched by our staff.

Here's how:

1. Visit *www.facthound.com*

2. Choose your grade level.

3. Type in this book ID **1429617144** for age-appropriate sites. You may also browse subjects by clicking on letters, or by clicking on pictures and words.

4. Click on the **Fetch It** button.

FactHound will fetch the best sites for you!

Index

Word Count: 104
Grade: 1
Early-Intervention Level: 12

Editorial Credits
Lori Shores, editor; Renée T. Doyle, set designer; Danielle Ceminsky, book designer;
   Wanda Winch, photo researcher

Photo Credits
Art Life Images/age fotostock/Jörgen Larsson, 4
Fiona Green, cat courtesy of Silver 'N Gold Cattery, Texas,
   cover, 8, 16, 18, 20
Peter Arnold/Biosphoto/J.L. Klein & M.L. Hubert, 6
Shutterstock/Anna Utekhina, 1, 10, 22
Ulrike Schanz Photodesign & Animal Stock, 12, 14